Gnomes

ps to make your own Tomtes
By Nora Begona

A *nisse* (usually Norwegian) and a *tomte* (usually Swedish) are similar characters. They are both solitary, mischievous domestic sprites responsible for the protection and welfare of the farmstead and its buildings. Tomte literally means "homestead man" and is derived from the word tomt which means homestead or building lot. Nisse is derived from the name Nils which is the Scandinavian form of Nicholas.

A tomte is described as an older, little man about the size of a young child. He wears old often ragged clothes, usually gray or navy, and sports a bright red cap on his head. He resides in the pantry or barn and watches over the household and farm. He is responsible for the care of the farm animals, especially the horses. The tomte or nisse has an enormous capacity for work but will not tolerate anyone's interference. It is believed that a clean and orderly home or farm is an indication that this domestic sprite resides there.

Tomtar and nisser require very little of the humans they work for. They demand only the respect and trust of the farmer and a bowl of julegrøt (Christmas porridge) with butter on Christmas Eve. These spirits will not remain in a home where respect is lacking and thus the farm will not thrive and the farmer will be reduced to poverty.

These are the authentic gnomes that can be found all over Scandinavia. They are the mythological creatures from Scandinavian folklore, typically associated with the winter solstice and the Christmas season. In Finland they are called Tonttu, in Sweden Tomte, and in Norway these little fellows go by the name of Nisse. Scandinavian folklore is rich with many types of woodland creatures, gnome or tonttu/tomten being one of them. They are believed to protect the family and animals from misfortune, and to bring good luck to you and your home. Even though these gnomes are traditional, they are simply adorable in a modern way. They go well with any home decor or any season.

Though I do not come from Nordic cultures, I have been nurtured around creativity and crafting, coming from a family with sewing enthusiasts, knitters, and woodworkers. Been surrounded by skill and creativity all my life, I unknowingly held a treasure of creating from a scratch from very early on. My goal is to create beautifully handcrafted, heirloom gnomes with personalities for gnome lovers around the world. I make the gnomes from start to finish by hand, and carefully select the materials I use for each gnome. We strive for perfectly constructed items, and it's indeed the handmade aspect that makes them truly unique. Each gnome is an individual and no two will ever be exactly the same.

So after all this introduction let's make some gnomes.

STEPS
1- Trace and cut your felt or fabric according to the template

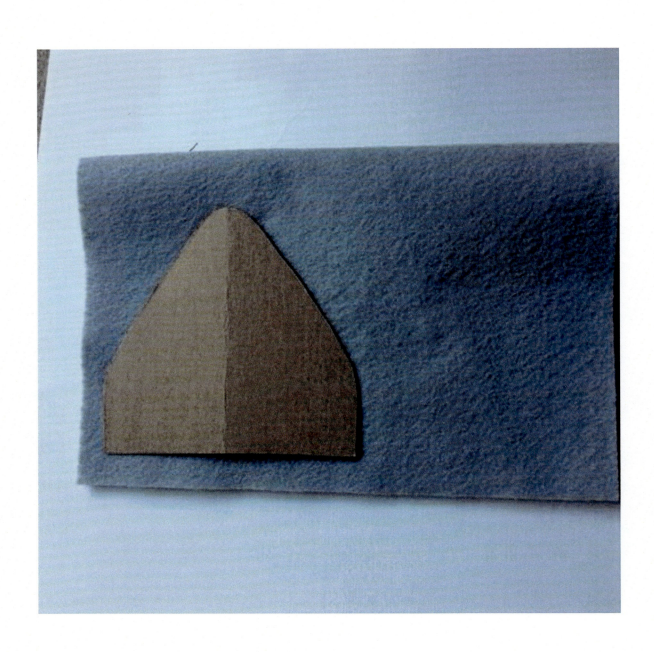

STEPS

1- Trace and cut your felt or fabric according to the template

STEPS

1- Trace and cut your felt or fabric
according to the template

2- Sew the hat together with zig-zag stich in your sewing machine.

3-Sew the body with a straight stich in the sewing machine

4- Attach the bottom with the same stich.

5-Make a cut in one of the sides of the body, and turn over the fabric. (do not worry, you will stich this cut, and it will be covered by the beard.

6- Get a stocking (you can buy a packet of ten at Walmart) cut it and place it around a glass or mug.

7-Place the stocking around a glass or mug.

8-Tie the end and make the bean bag.

9- Place the bean bag inside the gnome body.

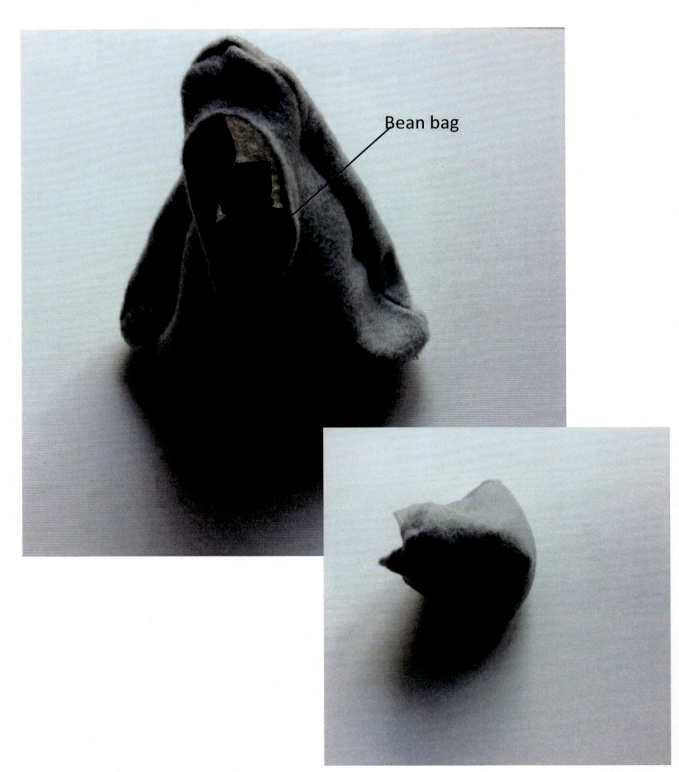

Bean bag

10- Fill in the body with poly fill . Be careful on the corners, it should be very well filled.

11- When the body is all filled, sew
the cut, with a cross stich.

Nose

12- Cut a small square from the same stocking and make a running stich all around, gather it a little bit, and fill it with poly fill. Start gathering harder, making a ball, not very round just kind of oval. Tie it thread all around many times and cut it.

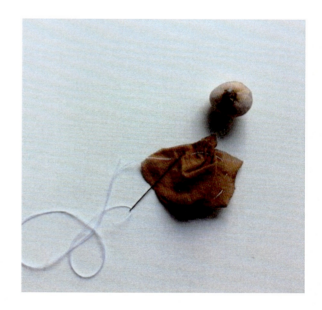

Nose

11- Cut a small square from the same stocking and make a running stich all around, gather it a little bit, and fill it with poly fill. Start gathering harder, making a ball, not very round just kind of oval. Tie the thread all around many times and cut it.

12- As regards beards, you can choose any kind of material.
I buy hair extensions. You have different types and price range. You can make them with frizzy hair or silky and straight., I guess it is a matter of tastes. I like both.

Cut a strip of felt and place it all along the width of the hair.

13- Sew with a zig zag stich, twice.

14- Place the beard all around the pointed edge of the body, sew or glue it.

15- Place the nose in the middle and glue it too.

16- Place glue all around the hat border, and glue it to the head. Take care to cover all the felt strip from the hair.

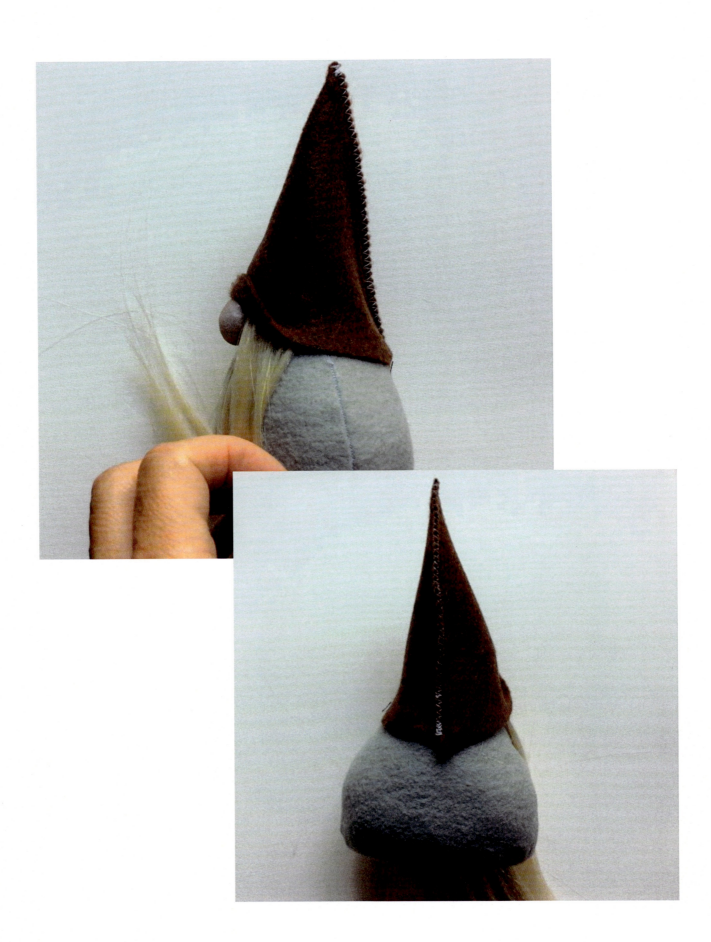

Tips:

This is a basic gnome of about 7 inches tall. You can add him embellishments, such as make a pair of braids on the bear, a knitted hat, a stack of sticks, whatever your creativity leads you.

Pattern

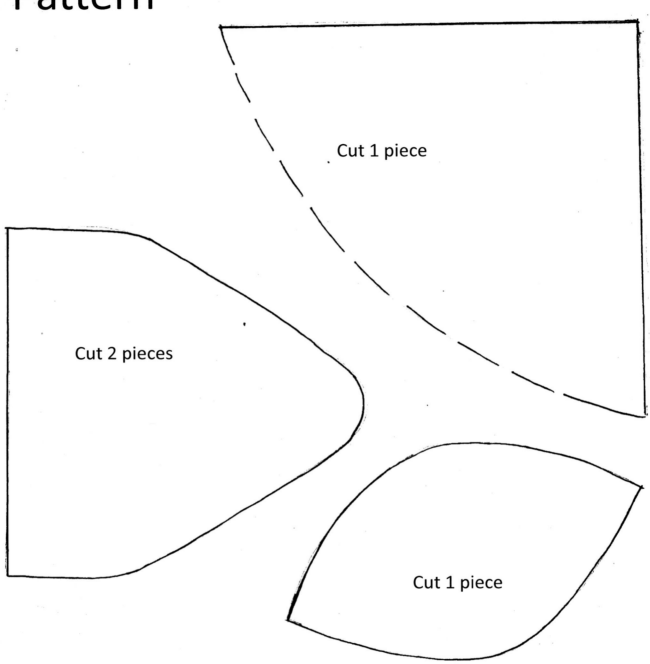

Cut 1 piece

Cut 2 pieces

Cut 1 piece

Hope you like this little creature, make a lot, have them around your house. I am sure they will make you smile.

If you like this craft, please visit once in a while my Etsy shop:

https://www.etsy.com/shop/mamatitina

Facebook Page:

https://www.facebook.com/blissmagic/

Twitter:

https://twitter.com/NoraBegona

Instagram:

https://www.instagram.com/nbegona

You Tube:

https://www.youtube.com/user/begonanora

My Blog:

http://mamatitina.blogspot.com/

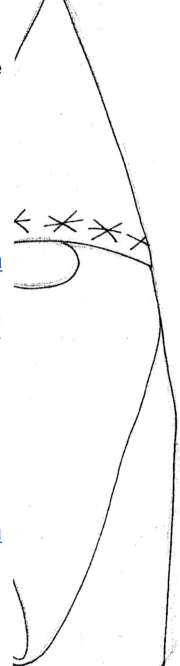

Thank you
Nora Begona
2016

Made in the USA
San Bernardino, CA
30 October 2018